THE ROAD BETWEEN US

A Father & Son Bicycle Route 66

CHRISTOPHER BRISCOE

Shifting Gears Productions
Ashland, Oregon
www.chrisbriscoe.com

THE ROAD BETWEEN US: A Father & Son Bicycle Route 66

Copyright © 2018 by Christopher Briscoe

All rights reserved. No part of this book may be reproduced in any written, electronic, recorded, or photocopied format without written permission of the publisher or author. The exception would be in the case of brief quotations embodied in critical articles or reviews and pages where permission is specifically granted by the publisher or author.

Photography by Christopher and Quincy Briscoe
Writing Consultants/Editors: Dorothy J. Best, Carolyn Bond, and Will Wilkinson
Interior and cover design by Jeff Altemus, Align Visual Arts

ISBN: 978-0-9899404-8-1

Printed in the United States of America

Dedication

To all the parents who wish they'd taken their child on an adventure and to all those who will after being inspired by this story.

CONTENTS

8   Fathers & Sons

18   Route 66

24   An Invitation

36   The Bicycle

48   The Prints We Leave Behind

56   Respect

64   Moving the Map

78   The Mojave

84   The Wind

90   Let's Make Some Friends

98   This Ain't No Air BnB

108   Almost Blacklisted on Route 66

116   My Name's Harley. Who the Hell Are You?

Easy Mornings 126

Where Hooters is a Family Restaurant 134

Missouri: Where Every Chicken Is Named Bob 148

Café Culture 158

On Our Way to Nowhere 166

When the Journey is More Important than the Destination 180

A New World Champion 188

Thirst 198

Crossing the Big Muddy 208

The End of So Many Things 220

The Wind in Our Sails 228

Postscript 236

FATHERS
— & —
SONS

— THE ROAD BETWEEN US —

M Y SON, QUINCY, SAW THE OLD COWBOY first. He was moving slowly down a line of fencing alongside the road, carrying a small coil of barbed wire, evidently looking for breaks. A rusting, cream-colored Chevy pickup was parked nearby in the dry scrub. The cowboy was tall, lean, and weathered, with a thick, white mustache. With gloved hands he was working the wire, twisting it, snipping it with care.

Quincy and I rolled off the highway up to the fence wire right across from the man. Two guys on packed bicycles must have been a head-scratcher for him. "How far is it to Santa Fe?" I asked.

He smiled. "You're almost there," he said, gesturing. "It's just down the road."

"So glad," I replied. "My son and I are bicycling from Los Angeles to Chicago. We've had a long day."

His brow lifted. "On those bi-cy-cles?"

HE TOOK OFF HIS GLOVES and hung them over the wire. "Archie West is my name," he said as he extended his hand. It was sandpaper rough.

He asked the questions that many have asked us along the way: How many miles do you do a day? Where do you sleep? How about those crazy drivers? How long do you think it will take you to get there? We answered. Then I said, "The best part about this trip is doing it with my son."

He smiled again. "My son recently moved back on the ranch. He's usually out here with me. I love working with my boy."

I asked about his ranch, how long he's lived there and if he raised any crops. Archie glanced at me. "This land is too dry to plant any crops. The only thing you can raise here is cattle." Using the sole of one boot, he scraped at the bare earth, pushing it aside, inspecting it. It was dry. "We finally had a big rain last night. It's never enough."

> *"It's mostly houses now. I may be the last stockman alive."*

HE STARTED TELLING QUINCY AND ME the history of his family, how his dad had settled here from Oklahoma just before the Dust Bowl Era, and how Archie had grown up on the ranch. "This land has been grazed for hundreds of years. I've run cows on a lot of this country. It's mostly houses now. I may be the last stockman alive."

It would have been easy to stay longer, but Quincy and I still had a few miles to pedal before dark. We waved good-bye and rolled on down the windy road, pedaling side by side.

The old cowboy turned back to working his fence, moving along the wire. The black-and-blue thunderstorm gathered and circled behind him, beyond the waiting pickup, unsettling the high desert dust.

ROUTE
—66—

— THE ROAD BETWEEN US —

THE ROAD SURFACE ON ROUTE 66 IS SEVERAL layers thick—one stacked on top of another like pages in a history book. One of the first layers was made by covered wagons heading west. After the wagon trains came the first automobiles, traveling on dirt, then on gravel.

— ROUTE 66 —

In 1915, Edsel Ford wanted to promote his Model T, so he drove it from Detroit to San Francisco, mostly along Route 66. He wrote in his trip log of concerns about "highwaymen" in the desert—robbers on horseback who would hold up travelers at gunpoint.

Every bump, every dip, every pothole becomes part of our brief moment…

IN 1926 CAME A TOPPING OF PORTLAND CEMENT that turned into what Steinbeck called the Mother Road—the escape route Oklahoma farmers took as they fled the Dust Bowl looking for work. Route 66 was decommissioned for a while. In the 70s, the interstate took over parts of it. On our trip, we chased it as much as we could, which meant occasionally bicycling on freeways, sometimes on frontage roads. Most of the time, we traveled on the original Portland cement road, much of which is now drizzled with black rivulets of tar, swirling and meandering, covering the cracks of time.

This layer is the one that matters to bike riders. It's the one we feel our tires roll over, spinning their song. Every bump, every dip, every pothole becomes part of our brief moment in the history of this road and belongs in the pages of this particular story of a father and his son who pedal their way from one end of Route 66 to the other.

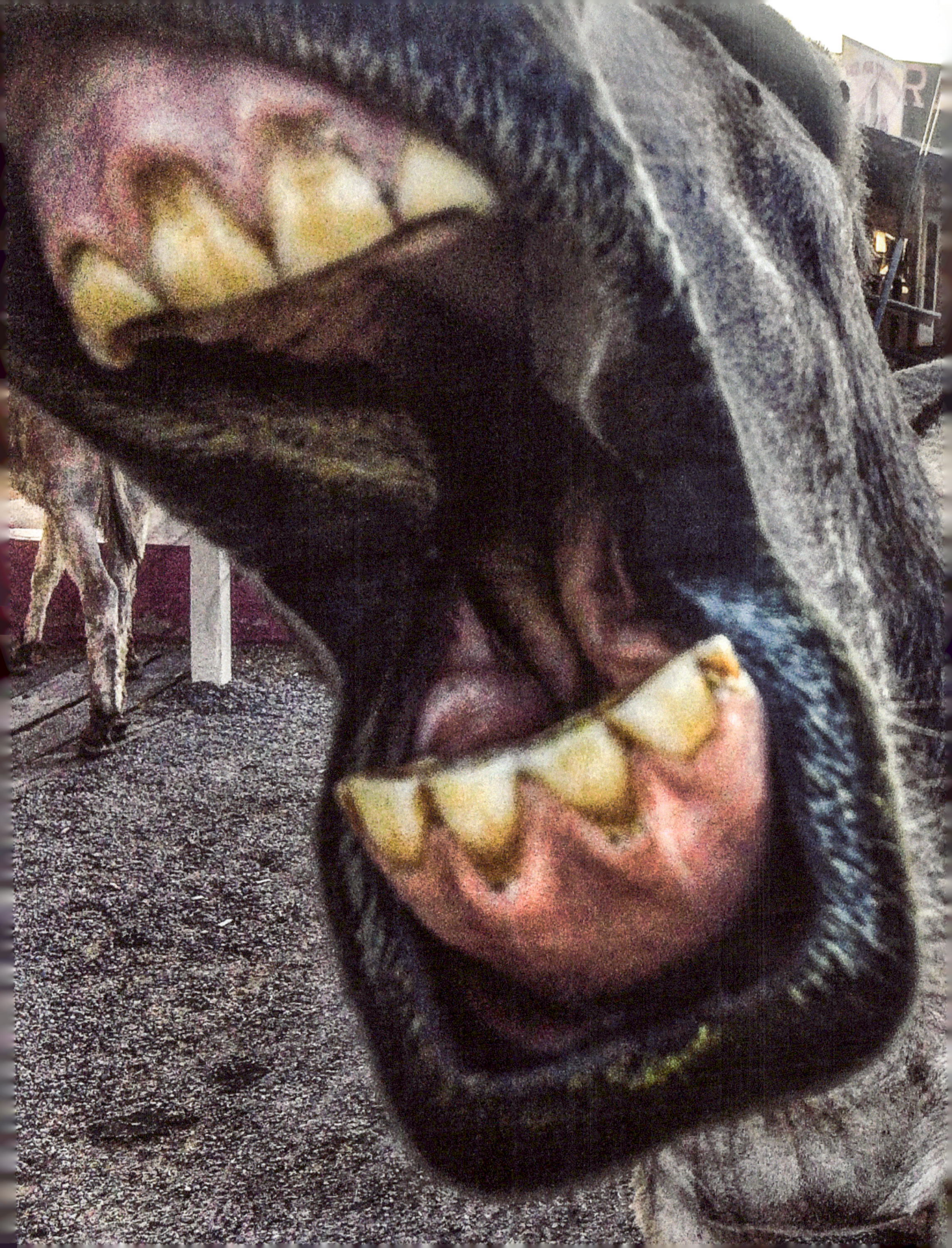

—an— INVITATION

— THE ROAD BETWEEN US —

BEFORE AUTOMOBILES RAN HORSES OFF ROADS, bicycles led the modern transportation revolution. The bicycle is the most efficient travel machine ever invented, the equivalent of the average car traveling 1,600 miles on one gallon of gas. Even aviation evolved from bicycle technology, as

the Wright Brothers were bicycle builders first. Besides fostering a technological revolution, the bicycle also provoked a social one—women's liberation. The bicycle was a gender equalizer. Women could travel solo. It gave them independence and a new freedom to travel more than a half day's walk from their home. Susan B. Anthony famously said, "I think the bicycle has done more to emancipate women than anything else in the world."

Currently there are more than a billion bicycles on the planet.

Most of us can remember learning to ride a bike as children, especially the first time we made it around the whole block. Nothing before that moment equaled the sense of freedom and joy we discovered on that bike. It was typically the first machine that we learned to master. As we got older we knew that it was also good exercise. Later still, when we found ourselves needing large bottles of Ibuprofen, our once-beloved bikes leaned idly in the garage.

MY FIRST BICYCLE RIDE ACROSS AMERICA was in 1976—our country's bicentennial. My buddy Brian Zahl and I pedaled more than four thousand miles, sleeping in baseball dugouts, in farmer's barns, in the home of a Wyoming sheriff, in a Kansas jail, behind Safeways, and later working on an Amish farm. We got by on $3.50 a day. We never broke our rule of not accepting even one offer of a ride. That adventure shaped the rest of my life and still resonates deep within my soul.

— AN INVITATION —

One summer day in 1978, another friend, Richard Tunzat, and I put our back tires in the Pacific Ocean off Newport, Oregon, and, at the end of that long summer, we dipped our front tires into the Atlantic off the tip of Cape Cod. A few years later, I soloed from my hometown, Ashland, Oregon, to Minneapolis, covering the two thousand miles in just 19 days.

There were many more bicycle treks during the following years—most of them two- to three-week trips. By the time I was close to turning 50, I felt the need to bike across the country again and pedaled from San Diego to the east coast of Florida.

Friends have often asked, "What was the most difficult part? Climbing the Rockies? Crossing the desert? The headwinds?" My answer always came easy and was always the same: the hardest part is simply getting on the bike and leaving town. It's quite the metaphor for so many other challenges.

TOURING THOUSANDS OF MILES on bike adventures has taught me to lean into the unfamiliar, welcoming whatever might nudge me out of my comfort zone: meet the resistance, embrace it, push through it, then transcend it. Taking a risk and moving forward does not require a passport. It requires saying "yes," especially when a considerable part of us wants to say "not now."

Around the year 2000, Photoshop, with the required computer,

Christopher Briscoe and Brian Zahl on the way to completing their 4,000-mile transcontinental trip in 1976.

became one of my professional photography tools. I put my bike up on a hook in the garage. For the next 16 years, instead of hunching over drop-down handlebars, I hunched over Steve Jobs's machine. My bicycle's only movement was gently swaying from a garage rafter as if from a hangman's noose.

My son, Quincy, grew up listening to my bike adventure stories. Barely out of high school, he rode his bicycle, alone in the winter, from Antibes, France, to Barcelona, Spain. Then he pedaled from St. Augustine, Florida, to San Diego—traversing the same route I'd ridden in 2000 but in reverse. That wasn't enough for him. A year later, he and his buddy Charlie Slattery biked from Alaska all the way to Mexico.

ONE DAY IN 2016, Quincy, now 23, suggested that we bicycle across America together on Route 66. The look in his eyes told me that he was serious. I smiled. I felt honored that my son would actually want to take such a long bicycle trip with his dad, but I was done with that chapter of my life. So, I put my arm around him and said, "Son, I've been over the Rockies four times. Now I'm fat, I'm tired, and frankly, I'm too damn old."

I remember heading across the room for the coffee pot, wincing at a familiar knee pain. Quincy stopped me. "Dad, we gotta do this together." My mind finished his thought, "...*before it's too late.*"

Christopher leaves on another solo bicycle trip in 1996.
Quincy points the way.

— AN INVITATION —

I'D ALWAYS ENCOURAGED MY SON to travel far from the rest of the herd. I'd done my best to model that behavior. But now, at 64, I was too far out on "the thin end of the branch" to survive, let alone enjoy, another bicycle adventure.

I shook my head as I lowered myself back into the weathered armchair that suddenly seemed a hundred years old. Older even than me.

I sat there awhile, sipping my coffee, barely noticing as it got cold. I was irritated, confused, distracted.

I didn't want to be the old guy on a bike at the bottom of the steep hill, panting, sweating, and cussing, while his 23-year-old kid waited impatiently at the summit, doing push-ups and thinking of a thousand other places he'd rather be. Yet I felt pulled to go, humbled by the fact that my son wanted to do it with me.

I was afraid of being weak—and I felt weak. I was afraid of failing in front of my son. Afraid of his seeing me as different from the dad he had admired for so long. After all, this was the most important relationship I'd ever had. I just couldn't risk fracturing it.

Quincy, right out of high school in 2012, leaves from Florida on his solo trip to San Diego.

the
BICYCLE

O NE SUNNY MORNING A WEEK OR SO LATER, I walked into Piccadilly Cycles, my neighborhood bike shop and, on a whim, asked if I could try out one of their electric-assist bikes. I planned to just pedal around the block.

I headed down the street. Weird—there seemed to be a brisk wind at my back. At the end of the block, I noticed that I didn't turn around; I barreled ahead. What's going on? Hills had become flatter. My legs seemed stronger. Suddenly, the fun of riding a bike was back.

I returned and slapped down a $200 deposit. When I told Quincy, he laughed. "Why don't you just buy it?" he asked. I was being financially prudent, I told him. His laugh told me that he figured maybe something else was going on.

MANY PEOPLE THINK AN E-BIKE is a fully electric bicycle. It's not. The Bosch system is brilliant. You don't just push a button and go. It requires you to pedal, and then it creates a perfect synergy among the effort your legs put out, the selected gear's efficiency, and the energy supplied by the small electric motor. I soon learned to coordinate shifting gears with moving among the four power levels of assistance. I thought, "This machine could become my new best friend."

Some traditional spandex-clad bicyclists sneer at e-bikes, as if diminishing the pain while enhancing the fun is somehow cheating. In 1903, Henri Desgrange declared, "Variable gears are only for people over 45. Isn't it better to triumph by the strength of your muscles than by the artifice of the derailleur? We are getting soft.…Give me a fixed gear." That guy founded the Tour de France.

I'm sure that horse-and-buggy riders sneered at the first automobiles. Traditional skiers scoffed at the first ski lifts, and early surfers ridiculed the first boards with leashes. Certainly, die-hard photographers initially scorned the advent of digital cameras. Progress always encounters resistance. When I asked a friend if he'd tried an e-bike, he scoffed, "I'm not that old yet."

I remembered his comment as I wrestled with my own resistance. Finally, after tiring of Quincy's badgering, I bought the bike.

Suddenly I was sweating. The speedometer flashed a big 25 at me, then 27, then 30…

I DECIDED TO EXPLORE THE BIKE'S LIMITS, so late one evening I pedaled up Morton Street, one of the steepest streets in my town, Ashland, Oregon. I had to work hard, and I discovered that my knees were the weakest link in the power train. Amazingly, however, I wasn't zigzagging but was going straight up. When I finally made it, I was tired but I wasn't dead. I turned around and headed downhill. My world shrank to the narrow path of light my headlamp spilled onto the pavement ahead as the bike accelerated. It was thrilling—until I applied the brakes. The bike slowed but didn't stop. I squeezed the brake levers hard into the handlebars, but I only gained more speed.

Suddenly I was sweating. The speedometer flashed a big 25

at me, then 27, then 30. I shot through one intersection, then another. I smelled the brakes burning and feared that soon the only usable brake pad left would be my face. I was heading toward a corner house. I could see some guy sitting in his living room watching TV.

I had a few choices: smash through his picture window, swerve right onto a dogleg and keep descending, or attempt a hard left turn onto a cross street that headed back uphill. Miraculously, I put one foot down, dragging it on the pavement, and somehow managed to make the 90-degree left turn. Now gravity became my best friend. I shuddered to a stop, shivering yet dripping sweat in the night air.

The bike shop installed a larger brake disc that we hoped would solve the problem.

SOON AFTER THAT ADVENTURE, I made the mistake of Googling bicycle trips and found myself watching a YouTube video of some poor fellow from South Africa telling how he had barely survived a 110-mile journey through the Mojave Desert. His water got so hot he couldn't drink it. His final words on the video rang in my head for days afterward: "I almost died out there."

He was in his twenties. I was a lot older and a lot more vulnerable.

However, for some reason beyond fear or logic, the more I encountered reasons to say no to Quincy, the more I felt compelled to say yes. Something had stirred within me that I couldn't ignore. I knew that the best adventures happen when you bite off more than you can chew and live through it.

"You're sure?" Quincy asked when I told him. "You really want to do this—with me?"

For a moment, I wondered if he'd only suggested the trip to be nice to his old man. No, he was serious. And so was I.

I REMEMBERED WHEN QUINCY first mastered riding a bike. He was barely six. I wrote him a letter the next day. I had been writing letters to him at key moments in his life since the day he was born, putting them in a shoebox for safekeeping.

March 7, 1999

Dear Quincy,

This past year, I have often taken you over to Garfield Park to ride your shiny red-and-yellow bike. A few months ago, we took the training wheels off. Like my dad did when I was a boy, I would run alongside you, holding on to the back of the bicycle seat as you wobbled over the sidewalk. You would make it just a few yards before laying the bike over on the grass, then getting up to try again. But yesterday was different.

It was a sunny morning. The fresh smell of the previous night's rain was still hanging in the air. A few families with children

— THE BICYCLE —

had spread out blankets on the damp grass. I ran along beside your bike, holding the back of the seat. After a few wobbly moments, you hollered, "Let go, Dad. Now, Dad, let go! NOW!"

A few feet on your own soon became several yards. You rolled farther down the sidewalk. I wanted to run after you, stay at your side, help you steer. But I stopped. "Let go!" you had cried. "Now."

I held my breath, tense, watching you nearly hit a pair of newly planted trees, then dodge an overflowing trash can, before you crashed. Luckily, the grass cushioned your fall. I resisted the urge to run and help. A few seconds later, you were back up, riding away.

You crashed again, and this time tears flowed. I moved to you now, in a few strides. A nasty bruise appeared on your forehead. I wiped your tears away, and you hopped back on your bike. "Quincy, remember to use your brakes this time!"

You rode another fifteen minutes, crash free. Then we sat together on a bench, your helmeted head against the side of my chest. "Quincy," I asked, "do you think someday you could make it all the way around this park without stopping?"

You scanned the route, then slowly nodded, serious and careful. A few moments later, you mounted your bike and started out along the familiar part of sidewalk that circles around the park, riding with confidence. Soon, the figure eight you had been tracing for weeks expanded. You crossed the basketball court, over a small patch of grass, then merged onto the sidewalk on your way to the Big Loop.

You hit the brakes (you remembered!), curved left, and made the first turn, then gunned it along East Main Street. After the next turn, your momentum waned as you struggled to keep your balance and make it back up the incline. I was standing high on my toes, straining to see, my eyes locked onto every pedal stroke, every wobble. Your handlebars lurched from side to side, but your little legs kept churning away, navigating the last corner. On the final straightaway, you looked up to make sure I was watching.

After completing the Big Loop once, you kept going, recircling that park until the sun began to set. Who cares if it's getting dark? How far did you want to go, Quincy? Perhaps all the way across America.

Back home after dinner, as you got ready for bed you pleaded, "Dad, please, can I wear my knee pads all night long?"

"Of course," I replied.

"Can I wear my elbow pads to bed, too?"

"Of course."

Love, Dad

NOW, AS THE NEW OWNER OF AN E-BIKE, I had the same kind of impulse. I remembered how, many years ago, I'd put my first Nikon camera on the pillow beside me so I'd see it when I woke up. John Lennon, as a kid, had put his first bike

— THE BICYCLE —

Quincy learns to ride a bike.

next to his bed. Keith Richards had slept next to his first guitar. If only I could get my e-bike under the covers.

Q UINCY AND I TALKED TIMING FOR THE TRIP, which was important. We'd have to find the ideal climate window: late enough in the year to avoid snow on the Great Divide and early enough to avoid the worst of the summer heat. The more we talked details, the more excited I became.

Game on.

So here it was: I would be riding 2,700 miles from Santa Monica to Chicago with my son. My prayer? That my legs wouldn't scream so loud that I'd remember my age. That this miraculous e-bike would narrow the fitness gap between a 64-year-old AARP guy and a 23-year-old macho kid. Best of all, that taking this risk would pay off in creating a mythic adventure with my son.

Quincy's first trans-continental trip from St. Augustine, Florida, to San Diego, California. 2012.

the PRINTS — we leave — BEHIND

— THE ROAD BETWEEN US —

I BECAME A PROFESSIONAL PHOTOGRAPHER four decades ago, and I almost always shoot portraits. Here's why.

When people flee a disaster, they rescue, in this order: family members, pets, and family photographs. People know they can replace "stuff," but if the photographs of a lifetime are gone, part of the family's history is gone. Neither money nor tears can replace them.

Someday, each of us will be gone too. Photographs help preserve our legacy; it's how future generations can know their ancestors. Photographs take on new significance when you think of them this way. Sometimes my phone rings and I hear: "Grandpa passed away recently, and you took the last photograph of him. Thank you!" Or worse, "My son died in a car wreck on Monday. I'm staring at the picture you took of him last year." Or, "My sister has terminal cancer. I want to bring her into your studio for one last photo."

People often ask if I shoot landscapes—to which I reply: "The greatest landscape is the human face." People don't carry pictures of landscapes in their wallets.

THE OTHER THING THAT IS IMPORTANT to me, besides freezing time, is being creative. I always want to push the boundaries to give my clients something they don't expect, reveal a side of them we might not always see.

One of my studio clients was a chef who wanted a professional resumé portrait. He showed up for his appointment, and I did what he expected. Then I suggested: "Hold this basket of eggs. Let's crack one on your head!"

A dad drove a few hundred miles for me to take a portrait of him with his baby. After his arrival, the baby would not stop crying. I knew I couldn't control the baby but I could direct the father, so I said, "Dad, you cry too!"

A house painter needed a photo for an ad. "Let's put you in a white tux and have one of your crew get up on that scaffolding and slowly pour a bucket of black paint over you."

Sisters in a high school portrait? They dressed up in flowing gowns, and I photographed them having a tea party—underwater. A doctor arrived for his portrait session and I found out that he specializes in headaches, so, naturally, I photographed him with a vice crushing his head. When a bride arrived, I turned on my rain machine. I convinced a symphony maestro to bicycle through a storm, no hands, with his tux on, conducting as he pedaled. The governor of Oregon needed a new photograph, and I asked him, "Can I stand on your desk, and can you lean back in your chair and put your cowboy boots up on the desk?"

When I was at Kirk Douglas's house, I handed his wife, Anne, a dog pooper scooper to hold into the camera. She did it, grimacing, as Kirk sat on a bench behind her and said, "Hey, there's more poop on the lawn that you missed!"

PORTRAITURE IS MY LIFEBLOOD as well as my canvas. It's also my olive branch to the universe. On a trip, and even sometimes in my hometown, I shoot "street photography."

When I see someone with a unique face, I often feel compelled, almost physically pulled, to photograph them. What I don't do next is snap and run. That would feel like taking something from them. Even asking "Can I take your picture?" would be like asking a new mother who doesn't know me, "May I hold your baby?" I might get permission, I might not.

Besides, it's not just the face and the photo that attract me. I am incessantly curious about people, about what makes them tick. We humans love to hear each others' stories, and most of us, when asked, love to share ours.

TRUST IS THE BEDROCK OF WHAT I DO. Without trust, my shooting style might be unsettling. I strike up a conversation. I build layers of trust. I might chat with someone for twenty minutes before even mentioning that I'm a photographer. Often I don't even say I'm a photographer. I'll just say, "You have a wonderful face—can I take your picture?" By now, they feel appreciated, and they understand that I want to snap their photograph simply to celebrate their character.

As I packed for this trip with Quincy, I knew we'd meet more than a few interesting people I'd want to photograph. What camera should I bring?

I left my bulky Canon 7D at home, along with the heavy Canon lenses. Instead, I packed my Sony A6000 mirrorless with 3 small lenses: a 18–55mm, a fish-eye, and a 70–150mm zoom. As a backup, I also packed a pocket-size Panasonic Lumix G with a 12–32mm zoom.

THE BEST CAMERA IS OFTEN THE ONE that's in your pocket. Much of the time, I just used my iPhone. Amazingly, the still images are always sharp, with enough pixels to enlarge prints beyond 11"x14". After a few weeks on the road, I purchased an iPhone slide-on lens ideal for the selfies we took while riding.

At home, I work with Photoshop every day. Reluctantly, I left my MacBook Air behind and packed my iPad instead. It was perfect for the trip. I used the snap-on keyboard to write and edit several of the stories in this book.

At the end of every day, I'd plug my card reader into the iPad and upload images. Editing photos was a blast with the (free) Snapseed app, which did 90 percent of what I needed. I found other apps that do remarkable feats faster and more efficiently than I can do on my studio desktop computer.

All this wonderful technology helped me bring together words and photographs to tell the tale of my adventure with my son along Route 66.

RESPECT

IT'S MAY 1ST. THE WEATHER IS WARMING, and the rains have almost left Southern Oregon. I'm riding my bike down B Street in Ashland, pedaling through the night. The moon is so bright that if I was wearing a headlight, it wouldn't make much difference.

I'm not riding the shiny, high-tech Felt bicycle I'll be taking on the trip. I'm riding my old mountain bike that's so scratched I can barely read the Gary Fisher decal on the down tube. I bought the bicycle when my now 23-year-old son was just three. This bike is as comfortable as an old rocking chair.

IT'S SINKING IN THAT IN JUST TWO WEEKS, I'm going to begin an almost 3,000-mile bicycle adventure with my son. We'll have a long stretch of more than 100 miles in the Mohave Desert with nothing resembling shade.

I think about the many preparation considerations as I ride. You never know where you'll be when the sun sets, so you carry your home with you—providing it can all be stuffed into four bike panniers. I've visited our local REI sporting goods store often. A lightweight sleeping bag and pad were obvious purchases. Water bottles and a Camelback are essential. I'll pack just two T-shirts, two pairs of underwear, and a couple pairs of socks. Hopefully, we will be washing clothes every evening. Little extras are gold, like the rechargeable battery that can power lights as well as a cell phone.

Less obvious things can be vitally important. Forget just one and you can find yourself in trouble and stranded. I think back to my 1980 trip, when two of my spokes broke in the middle of Nowhere, Idaho. I had been smart enough to tape spares to my bike tube, but not smart enough to realize that the spoke nipples could vibrate off. They had. And I hadn't packed spoke nipples.

I WALKED MY BIKE A FEW MILES ALONG a lonely farm road. My front brake levers were wide open so the wobbling front wheel could pass between them. I spotted a rancher mending his barbed wire fence and brought out my map to ask how far it was to town. "About 60 miles," he said. He looked down at my bent wheel and added, "They got a bike shop there, but everything 'cept the café is closed on Sunday." When I explained that all I needed was a couple of spokes, he smiled with an idea. "Yesterday I picked up part of an old bicycle at the dump. Why don't we go over to the house and have a look?" On top of his junk pile was a rusty bicycle wheel. The spokes were the perfect size—go figure.

Life on the road is like that. Preparation is vital. So is trusting in the kindness of strangers.

I keep riding through the moonlight down B Street, feeling a breeze on my face, thinking about the rigors of the journey ahead. At my age, 64, I should be training hard every day, right? Bicycling these six blocks should be good enough, right?

I slowly take my hands off the handlebars and relax them at my side. The asphalt rattles the bike as I ride the neighborhood street. I pass the bungalow-style homes—some with their porch lights on, some with the blue-gray glow of a TV pulsing inside, some dark and silent.

I close my eyes and continue pedaling. I try to count to 10 before I crash. I only make it to 8 before feeling compelled to open my eyes, but I don't crash.

FOUR DAYS LATER, QUINCY AND I MEET on the Santa Monica Pier, the bottom end of Route 66. We get a late start that first day and ride through the streets of Los Angeles, jockeying for the front position all day. At a stoplight, some guy rolls down his car window and asks where we're going. "Chicago? Man, I wish I could do that."

Half an hour later, we stop for a break in a donut shop. While we're there, a man walks up to us. "I saw you guys a few blocks back and thought, 'Those guys have ADVENTURE written all over them.' Where you goin'?"

We smile, as we would smile often at that question on the miles ahead. "Chicago? On those bikes? Wow! Yeah, I sure do wish I could do that!"

We log only 24 miles that first day before retiring to a funky motel on the outskirts of LA and heading to the nearby 7-Eleven for dinner. Later that night, we think we hear gunshots. Instead of freaking out, we just shrug, accepting it as part of the adventure.

Before nodding off, we talk about the people we've already met, including the donut shop guy and his obvious respect for our journey. This turns into a discussion about Aretha Franklin's "Respect," which might be the best R&B song of all time.

Isn't that what we all want—just a little respect? Isn't that why we're on Facebook and Instagram, and why we load up our iPhones with social media sites? We chase the "likes" and feel good inside when the digital high-fives pop up. But that's not the same as someone telling you that "you have adventure written all over you."

"What you need, baby, I got it. R-E-S-P-E-C-T..."

MOVING
—the—
MAP

— THE ROAD BETWEEN US —

IT'S OUR SECOND DAY. WE'RE EATING tall stacks of pancakes at an IHOP when someone from a Harley touring group sitting at a nearby table asks, "Are those your bicycles out there leaning against the window?"

"Yep," Quincy says. "We're biking Route 66, all the way to Chicago."

— MOVING THE MAP —

When they hear that, some of them jump up and want to take our photos. That feels good, but it feels even better when Quincy announces: "The best part of this trip is that I get to do it with my pops."

SOME HOURS OF PEDALING through the city later, I spot a Starbucks and we take another break. Quincy lies down for a nap on the cement patio outside the front door. He wouldn't do that in our hometown, but on a trip like this, the rules are different. The previous day, we rested near the back door of a dapper downtown brokerage firm and attracted the attention of a security guard, who seemed puzzled to learn that we weren't homeless. In other words, if we weren't homeless, why were we lying on the walkway taking a nap?

The road inspires this kind of simplicity. Rest when you're tired, right where you are; no permission and no apologies required.

"Hey," I say when Quincy awakens, "why don't we just go from one Starbucks to another, all the way across America!" He rolls his eyes.

When Quincy wants to push us on, he plays a motivation game with me. It took me a while to wise up to his strategy. I call it "moving the map."

"Good news. There's another Starbucks coming up, just 10 miles," he promises. Then, as we near it, he says, "Hey, let's keep on

going, there's another one in 6 miles. Let's bang out 6 more—that's just 2 sets of 3."

I remember when I first encountered Quincy's ability to set goals for himself. As a baby, he would support himself on all fours, slowly rocking back and forth. He was ready to crawl but unsure exactly how to do it. One morning, I lay on the floor next to him and placed a magazine on the carpet just out of his reach. His eyes locked on it, his body started rocking; he wanted that magazine! I moved it closer. He rocked harder and then reached out to touch it. I moved it a few inches farther away. He rocked again, moving his right hand, then his left, determined to get to the magazine. I moved the magazine again. Undeterred, he rocked and moved forward toward his goal. My son was crawling!

TWENTY-TWO YEARS LATER, Quincy is moving the magazine on me. He keeps the maps and tells me how far we have to go to our next destination, but he rarely gives me absolute miles. After pedaling a couple of hours, I'm sure we've gone that far and ask how many miles are left. "It's just up the road, Dad." Somehow, the 15 miles he told me about turns into 20. Or more. He does this along our entire ride.

It works. The miles flow by steadily under our spinning wheels as we reach the edges of greater Los Angeles and our first serious challenge—the horrendous climb out of San Bernardino and over Cajon Pass.

Quincy is ahead of me on the shoulder, confronting the climb as we grind our way up Interstate 15. The City of Angels and the Pacific Ocean are far behind us. The mountains surrounding us are often cooked by fierce Santa Ana winds that can whip up raging wildfires. Winter storms can be nasty enough to force the Highway Patrol to close the pass down.

There are at least six freeway lanes abreast, weaving upward together—a river of cement covered with cars and semitrucks, like schools of migrating fish, all in a contest to make it over the pass. The Porsches glide effortlessly, small, shiny, and smooth. The semitrucks struggle under their own gluttonous weight, belching black smoke from their pipes, engines heating, threatening to give up the fight. Some portions of the railroad tracks through here are so steep that trains have lost the struggle, resulting in several train disasters through the years.

UNDERNEATH THIS WHOLE SCENE LURKS the San Andreas earthquake fault. A crack in the earth several miles deep, it snakes its way through California, vibrating and hungry, as if waiting to swallow everything up in one final gulp.

I fall behind, fighting oxygen debt like a clogged vacuum cleaner. Ahead of me, Quincy is standing up in his pedals. He looks just like I did at his age, riding with the same posture and same rhythm. He keeps his head down and pounds out the long stretch toward the summit. His shirt is off, his skin, partially

covered by the narrow trunk of his Camelback, browning under the California sun.

A long, dark shadow moves over me like a beast. I'm soon in a diesel cloud with a lung full of exhaust. The beast, pulling twin trailers, continues in the slow lane, closing in on my son. Quincy's bike suddenly shudders, smacked by a blast of wind from the passing predator. It downshifts to a crawl next to my boy, with tires like black ferris wheels, threatening to tug him in and chew him up. I watch closely, wanting to somehow sprint ahead and get between him and the truck. As if with cat's whiskers, Quincy intuitively senses the distance between his left shoulder and the wheels of the semi and carefully threads the needle between it and the guard rail. I let out a sigh. Although I'm relieved, a wave of sadness washes over me. I'm reminded that I'm not even slightly in control of my son's destiny.

Surrendering is hard to do.

IT SEEMS LIKE JUST FEW YEARS AGO—he may have been five – that my boy announced, "Dad, I want to climb a mountain." We went to the Outdoor Store in our little Oregon town and bought a pair of kid's leather hiking boots. He then counted down the days until the weekend.

It was in the middle of a damp Northwest winter. His mom packed us a lunch and made sure his coat was zipped all the way up. Quincy and I drove through the neighborhoods and wound our way past the city park to a small rock quarry. A narrow, bulldozed road angled up the side of a steep bank toward a ridge. My young boy took my hand, and the two of us walked through the damp air up the wet dirt road. His new hiking boots were soon covered with wet clay. He let go of my hand, picked up a rock, and hurled it over the edge. We cheered as it splashed into a large mud puddle below. We hiked on.

About 15 minutes into our big ascent, Quincy was tired. "Dad, can we sit down and have one of Mom's peanut butter and jelly sandwiches?" We chose a log to rest on that wasn't muddy. He opened the brown paper sack and brought out the halves of our sandwiches. Then he unfolded a small scrap of paper with a big red heart drawn on it—a sweet gift from his mommy. "Look, Dad," Quincy smiled and then held up two Oreo cookies Mom had also tucked into his bag. "Can I eat this first, before my sandwich?" Quincy smiled, offering me the other cookie as bribe.

"Why not?" I accepted his offer and bit the cookie in half. A small piece of it crumbled, falling into the mud. I glanced over to watch as he held his black-and-white Oreo cookie, slowly turning it with his tiny fingers, admiring the design, as if it were one of the wonders of the world.

At that moment, I knew one thing for sure: sitting on a decaying log in the Oregon mist, pretending to be on a climb up Mount Everest with my five-year-old son was the best wonder of my world. I needed nothing more in my life than to be with my son and two small cookies.

HALFWAY UP CAJON PASS, WE STOP AT a McDonald's where the highway crosses the Pacific Crest Trail. We join a throng of hikers who've paused to rest, recharge themselves and their phones. The place has only one power outlet, so they rotate their smart phones, sharing stories, trading food, and going into the restroom to wash socks.

We overhear talk about blisters, packing techniques, gear comparisons, and admiring tales of speed hikers who clock 50 miles a day. Tables are strewn with granola bars and chocolate, fair game for barter among hikers who've grown tired of their own snacks. A few of them debate resting a night or two at the Best Western across the road.

We form an instant community of twenty-first-century explorers—two adventure streams sharing a single reason for being on the move. It's the thrill of the journey, the camaraderie, and the pride that comes from stretching beyond the limits of what we thought was possible.

We say farewell to the hikers and head back to the shoulder of the crowded freeway, pedaling upward. I am beyond grateful for my bike's electric motor, giving me a reprieve from the decline of my lazy body during the past decade, reassuring me that I might eventually reach the summit.

At the top, a gentle breeze glides over the summit to cool me, as if to congratulate me: "You made it."

—the—
MOJAVE

— THE ROAD BETWEEN US —

O UR BICYCLES MOVE SLOWLY over the old sand-swept road. Lizards the color of the sand dart between dry scrub and disappear into sandy gullies washed smooth by flash floods. The desert spreads out right beyond the handlebars of my bicycle, like a carpet unrolling. The view is so

— THE MOJAVE —

wide that I can see the curvature of the earth, while the fireball in the cloudless sky bakes everything in sight. It's clear that we are visitors here.

Looking out over the miles of sand and rock, I mention, "Quincy, I can't imagine what it was like for the pioneers to struggle over this desert. What if they didn't time their trip right and ended up here in the middle of summer, when it's 120 degrees? Their wagons were pulled by mules or oxen. They only made about 15 miles a day. When they struggled over the mountains, they sometimes measured their daily progress in yards, not miles."

"Dude (my son often calls me "dude"), "that would be one epic adventure."

Just the thought of it made me reach for my water bottle.

the WIND

— THE ROAD BETWEEN US —

W IND CAN BE OUR FRIEND AND OUR FOE all in the same hour. It swirls itself around our bicycles as we move through it, with it, pushing it, caressed or nudged by it, and when we're lucky, carried by it. The wind has its own mind, and our welfare never figures into its thinking.

— THE WIND —

When it punches us in the face, we lower our heads and charge into it like bulls headed toward the matador. But we learn fast that this is a fight we cannot win. We hunch our shoulders over the handlebars to minimize the torture and grind it out. We keep our eyes down, staring at the pavement just ahead of the spinning front tire, as if ignoring the wind might make it go away.

We accelerate and smile, our spirits soaring...

Passing trucks interrupt our ordeal. They plow through the wall of wind for us, but every reprieve is brief. After a semi passes by, the wind smacks us with an even harsher blast. It feels like revenge, and we slow to a crawl. In those long moments, I often chance a quick glance up the road, hoping to see a sharp bend ahead that will shift the gale around to our side. Most of the time there's no bend, no consolation, so we dig deeper and keep on fighting.

If we see the clouds ahead churning, signaling a change in the weather, we start to bargain. There are times, not many, when the wind seems to hear us and take pity, moving around from a beam reach to a full gale off our stern. That's when our enemy becomes our best friend. Now we sit up tall, wishing we could hoist a colorful spinnaker and set sail. We accelerate and smile, our spirits soaring as we're blown down the highway like two happy ships sailing above the world.

LET'S MAKE SOME FRIENDS

— THE ROAD BETWEEN US —

MOST MORNINGS, BY THE TIME WE START OUT I'm in a great mood. Quincy needs a bit more time to wake up. As we pedal along the nearly empty roads side by side, I chatter and he just rides. Often, around 10 a.m., he politely tells me that he's going "under the white cloud." "Listen, it's not quite 10 yet," I bargain, as if that really matters.

— LET'S MAKE SOME FRIENDS —

"It's 10 o'clock somewhere!" he laughs and plugs in his white earbuds, connected to his iPhone music library. Those are the moments when I wish I had brought along a pair of hedge clippers so I could snip the cord. Quincy knows this and carries a spare, just in case I get inventive.

This becomes a daily ritual, so I try to squeeze in as much conversation as possible while there's still sand in the hourglass— before the clock strikes 10. Or I employ another strategy.

"Today, Quincy, we have just one goal: Let's make some friends! In fact, our goal today is to meet two new people!" Quincy rolls his eyes, knowing that "making friends" also involves chatting with them, taking their portraits, and maybe shooting a short video. He'd rather be under the "white cloud" listening to—heck if I know, but I'm certain it ain't Sinatra.

ON THIS TRIP, "FRIENDS" SHOW UP everywhere. We meet some character wandering down the blacktop in the desert picking up trash, a waitress and a fry cook in a crowded Missouri Waffle House, a guy in St. Louis who spotted us biking through the pouring rain. His name is Bill Mclean. We exchange Facebook info, and that evening we saw his post:

> *SO, IN THE MIDDLE OF one of the biggest downpours we've had around here in a while, I'm standing outside the hotel when this old guy rides by on a bike and asks where*

— LET'S MAKE SOME FRIENDS —

Starbucks is. This is not your normal bike. This one has side bags on it; it's really loaded down. I point across the street and say, "There ya' go."

Then a second guy rides by, he looks like a kid. "Thanks," he says. "We're cycling from LA."

It takes me a second for that to register. I walk over through the rain and ask them for a picture. Come to find out they're on their way to Chicago, heading along Route 66. And get this, they're father and son. How frigging cool is that?! Like, I had one of the best times of my life just playing golf with my son for the first time this week. I can only imagine how incredible this trip has to be for these guys.

Hey, Quincy – the kid's name is Quincy Briscoe – you and your father got me all hyped up. Two inspiring dudes out on one long bike ride. Safe travels, fellas!

That's one of the fantastic things about this trip—realizing that the opportunity to make friends is everywhere. I sometimes feel like a little kid walking up to another kid to ask, "Hi. What's your name? My name is Chris. Wanna be friends?"

EVERYONE IS A CHARACTER ALONG ROUTE 66, or perhaps we see them that way because we're just passing through. Here's the weird thing: The towns we live in for years are filled with interesting people too, strangers who could become friends as easily as they do out here. So why is it that some vagabond wandering down Route 66 picking up trash is a fascinating character, while the homeless guy sprawled in front of our hometown bank is a pain in the ass? It's worth thinking about.

A lot of transcontinental bikers who want to live in the "big chainring" don't take much time to meet interesting people along the way. For them, it's all about banging out the miles. Some may have jobs pulling on them, so they crank out 96 miles a day, treating their trip as just another rush to the finish line, then scurry home to the office. Why not just get on a treadmill and stay put? It's not the miles in your life that count, but the life in your miles.

Like the guy with the shotgun we met when we were desperate for a place to sleep overnight.

this
AIN'T
no
Airbnb

— THE ROAD BETWEEN US —

I**T'S THE END OF A DAY, OUTSIDE KINGMAN, ARIZONA.**
Quincy and I are fried. Grateful to find a gas station convenience store for a dinner of donuts and chocolate milk, we ask about a place to sleep. The owner directs us a few miles up the road. "There's a guy who's got some trailers, and he charges 10 bucks," he tells us. "Just look for the A-frame building on the left."

We push on through a strong wind. The sun begins to set as we roll through the desert, sure that a 10-buck trailer will be a lot better than a wind-rattled tent surrounded by grit and snakes.

A full six miles later, we reach the A-frame and knock on the door. No one home. We see a meandering row of trailers out back, stark in the fading light, and hear a freight train in the distance blowing its horn. We wander among the trailers, looking for signs of life, keeping an eye out for rattlers.

A DOOR POPS OPEN AND BANGS into the siding. An older man stands in the doorway and looks us over carefully. After a long, silent moment, he hobbles down the trailer steps, clinging to the railing, and extends a hand.

Charles has a handsome, chiseled face, with a trim, gray beard and a tightly rubber-banded ponytail. He smiles, revealing a few missing front teeth. He looks at our loaded bikes and asks a string of questions, each one flavored with the distinct smell of beer breath. I notice a large carton of beer on the kitchen floor past the open door and wonder how he lost those teeth.

Charles invites us in and offers us a beer. We settle into some old chairs. There's a pile of tobacco and a ragged hand-rolled cigarette on the countertop. I notice a scribbled sheet nearby. It's his monthly budget.

Personal – $10
Stamps – $5
Photos – $10
Booze – $200
Tobacco – $60
Savings – $100

You can tell a whole lot about a man from a piece of paper like that.

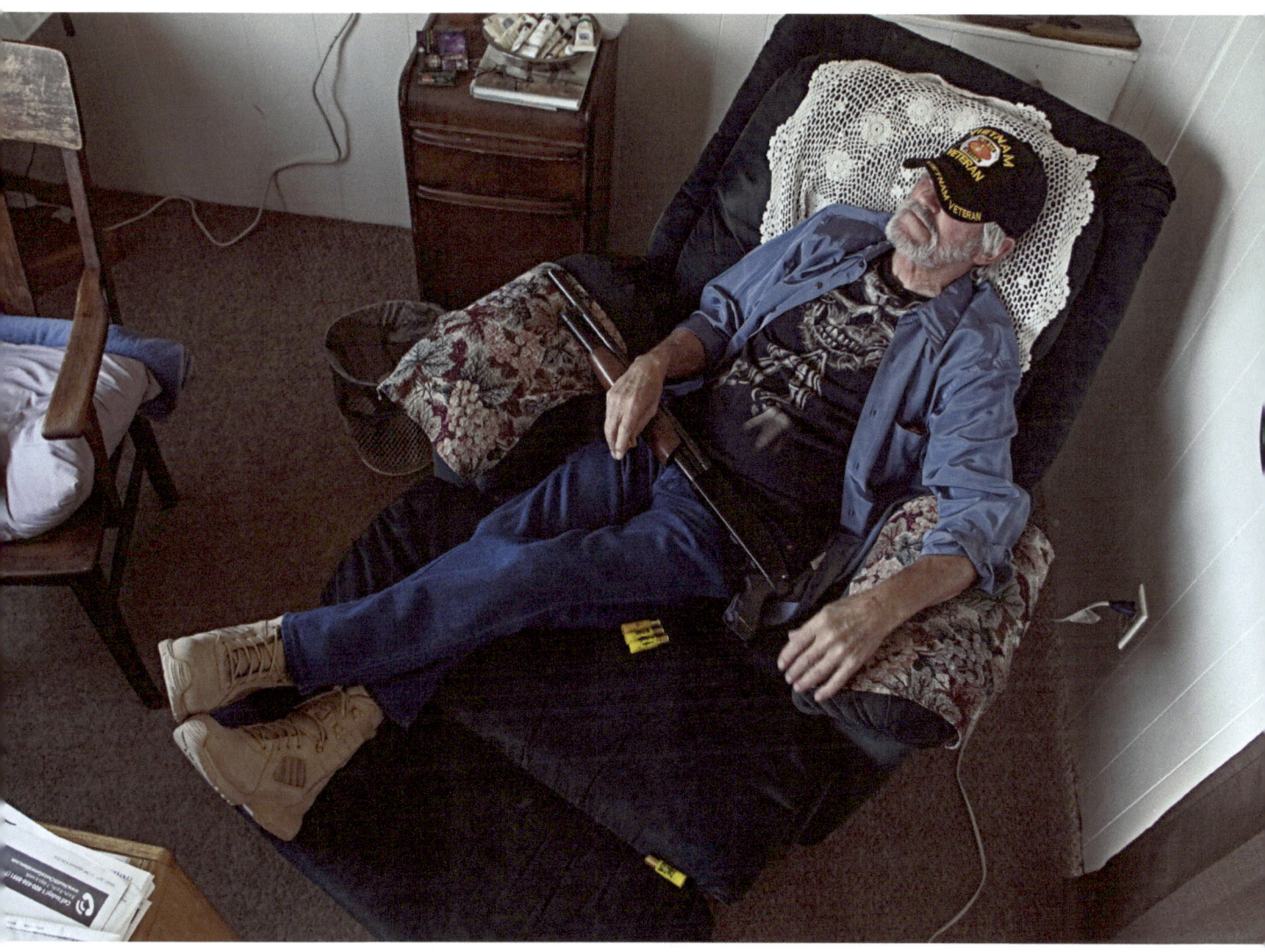

We learn that the owner of the trailer park is gone. I can tell that Charles is weighing options, figuring out how he can help us. After a few moments he says, "Okay. So, the only place for you to stay is here—in my trailer. That's the way it is. You two can have my bed, and I'll sleep in this recliner here."

Quincy and I exchange a silent glance: "Should we do this? Really?"

It's getting dark, and this is the only game in town. In fact, there is no town. We bring our bikes into the trailer and maneuver them into the cramped kitchen space that separates the bedroom from Charles's sitting room.

"LOOK AT THIS VIEW I'VE GOT," Charles says proudly, pointing out the side window. We peer through the shadows, wondering what he sees. "I asked my brother to come visit. I told him all about the animals I see out my window. It's the best view in the world! I told him I'd even give him my bed. He never came."

Charles directs us to the tiny bathroom. "Go ahead and use the shower, but make sure to put the plug back into the drain when you're finished. It empties out onto the desert floor and there's critters that like to crawl in."

Next he shows us the bedroom. A double mattress takes up most of the room. Sheets, blankets—we don't think too much about the details. We just want to get some sleep.

"You guys take my bed," he says again. "I'm gonna sleep down the hall in my Lazyboy." Charles reaches down next to the bed to retrieve his 12-gauge shotgun and a box of shells. "I'll just take these with me."

Quincy and I look at each other, uneasy with the notion of spending the night with a stranger holding a shotgun. Then we shrug, both of us thinking the same thing: "It's part of the adventure."

Charles sifted through a lifetime of possessions... left Indiana, and headed west.

A LOT OF FOLKS WHO LIVE WAY OUT HERE—some call them desert rats—just want to be forgotten. They're old. Social Security gives them just enough to manage. They like to be alone. Charles is one of them. Three marriages, two adult daughters who don't talk to him, and a mountain of bills. A few years back he broke his right ankle and it never healed correctly, so walking became painful. And finding work was difficult. He talks in a soft voice, looking down. "Do you think my daughters stepped up to help? Nope. Nothing. Not a damn thing."

We learn that his brother did—just handed him a four-grand wad of cash one day and said, "Go start over." So Charles sifted through a lifetime of possessions, loaded what was left into his car, left Indiana, and headed west. He's been here ever since.

Quincy and I are exhausted and have no trouble falling asleep. We wake up at six, our sunburned legs stiff. We find Charles sitting in his recliner wrapped in a blue bathrobe, smoking a cigarette and sipping coffee. He takes a drag and grins his toothless smile. "I'd offer you some coffee, but I only have one cup."

He asks if we want to hang out for a while longer, and we feel his loneliness. We've grown to like Charles, but the sun is up now and the heat will follow. We need to be on our way, and we figure we'll find a big breakfast down the road. We thank him for his kind hospitality and organize ourselves to leave.

CHARLES STANDS IN THE DOORWAY AND WATCHES us ride away. I glance back and wave as he closes the door and, I imagine, returns to his recliner to resume his favorite pastime: looking out into the desert through that side window. Maybe he's watching for animals and birds. Maybe he's scanning the horizon for the storms that roll in.

I keep thinking about Charles as we pedal. He lives alone in that metal box. That's his home, warmed by the sun and rocked by the wind. I can bet that he's still sitting there, maybe with his shotgun on the table along with a few rounds and a shopping list, sipping coffee from his only cup, and wishing that his daughters or his brother would give him a call. Overhead, a hawk circles, free in the wide blue sky.

almost BLACKLISTED — *on* — ROUTE 66

FRANKLY, I DON'T MIND CAMPING OUT, but at the end of a long, hot day on a bike, walking into an air-conditioned motel room and flopping down onto clean, cool, crisp sheets is a real oasis moment. It also means we can wash our clothes.

Quincy usually does his in the motel sink. I prefer the tub, tossing my dirty clothes in as it fills, squeezing in a free packet of motel shampoo, and stirring it around. Not perfect, but good enough. Then I drain the tub, turn on the shower, rinse the clothes under the spray, and give them a hearty wring-out. Finally, I spread the lot over the top of the shower curtain rod to dry. Most mornings, they're never dry and never completely clean.

WE WERE IN A MOTEL IN A LITTLE TOWN called Seligman in northwestern Arizona when I decided to MacGyver the situation. You may remember MacGyver from the TV show by the same name—my favorite as a kid. That guy could use any odd thing to get himself out of a jam. My MacGyver moment arrived that morning, when I decided that the microwave could become a clothes dryer.

My damp socks became my test run. I laid them out on the glass plate inside the microwave and set the timer for 30 seconds. Round and round they went. The light inside put a spotlight on the socks, as if they were circus performers under the Big Top. When the timer dinged, I popped open the microwave door. Dank steam wafted out, reassurance that my brilliant idea was working. I was thrilled. I'd invented something we could rely on for the rest of the trip. My socks—and these were the special ones I'd bought at REI for the trip—were hot and steaming, but not quite dry enough. I was sure another 30 seconds would do it.

Quincy wasn't so sure. "Dad! That's enough time. Don't put them in again!"

I was MacGyver, I had this. "It's okay, son, just a few more seconds will do it! Watch and learn, son. Watch and learn."

Ninety seconds would probably be better I thought. Maybe 120, just to make sure.

I rushed back to the kitchenette, where smoke was now pouring from the microwave...

I placed the socks back inside with ritualistic grace, laying them out like two strips of fatty bacon. I spun the timer to two minutes and punched the button. Since checkout time was nearing, I got busy packing up my bike, filling my water bottles, being careful as always to not leave anything behind, humming proudly.

"Dad!" I heard Quincy shout, and a half second later the smell hit me. I rushed back to the kitchenette, where smoke was now pouring from the microwave, releasing a cloud of Chernobyl-strength toxins into the room. I flung open the door and coaxed out the remainder of my socks with the hook of a clothes hanger. They had mostly sizzled into bubbling black goo.

My MacGyver moment was over.

THE GOOEY SOCKS HISSED AND STEAMED. We could hear the housekeeper's cart rattling down the cement walkway outside our door. Panic took hold. We turned on the bathroom fan and opened all the windows, fanning at the smoky air with towels. The smoke cleared fast, but the stench of burned plastic seemed stronger, as if it were penetrating everything in the room.

I threw the bubbling black mess into the sink for a dousing. Frantic to get rid of the evidence, I considered flushing them down the toilet. Too risky. I visualized the small flood a clogged toilet would create and got a brief flash of Inspector Clouseau in a Peter Sellers movie. I must have really tapped into his genius because I ended up hiding the socks' remains inside my bicycle panniers. This proved to be yet another mistake, because all my clothes absorbed the smell.

But I didn't know that yet. I borrowed Quincy's pocketknife to scrape at the hardened acrylic on the microwave plate. We towel-fanned the air like Tai Chi masters on speed. We could hear the housekeeper working in the room next door and knew ours was next. Quincy tossed the room key onto the dresser, and we elbowed each other out the narrow door, struggling with our loaded bikes and heading off at the bicycle equivalent of warp speed, never looking back.

It took a few miles before we relaxed, with no one in pursuit, and then we began to laugh. If Quincy had needed any further proof that his old man wasn't perfect, I'd just given him a memory for the ages.

MY NAME'S HARLEY

who the hell are you?

ERICK, OKLAHOMA, BECAME A DOT on the map in 1901. Now it's another Route 66 town fallen on hard times. Constructing a freeway a few miles over was enough to turn once-booming travelers' stops into near ghost towns. As a woman in Arizona said to Quincy and me: once the bank leaves and the hardware store leaves, you know your town is slipsliding away.

We slowly zigzag our bicycles down Erick's empty main street. The day is already getting hot, and we need some shade and breakfast. A boy on a bike coasts down the sidewalk, eyeballing the strangers. "Where's a good place to get some breakfast?" I ask him.

He shrugs and replies, "In this town? I don't think there is any."

I look across the street and notice a café. "How about that place?" I ask.

He looks over at it and shrugs, "Oh, yeah."

That's not exactly a sterling recommendation, but we're hungry and decide to give it a whirl. We stash our bikes and swing open the door to find a waitress repairing a broken chair with a tube of Super Glue, the chair's parts all laid out on one of the tables. Quincy and I choose a spot and order pancakes with eggs.

THE ONLY OTHER FOLKS IN THE RESTAURANT—a rancher and his wife—sit at a nearby table nursing cups of coffee. I walk over and ask him about a guy in town named Harley. He looks at me from under the brim of his tan cowboy hat. He's already spotted our bicycles outside. "Where you two coming from on dem by-cycles?" When I tell him our story, he puts down his coffee and slides his chair back, as if needing more space to comprehend it all. Then he turns to point out the window to where Harley lives. "Right there on that corner—

— MY NAME'S HARLEY. WHO THE HELL ARE YOU? —

the old red brick building with all dem signs all over it. He's different," he tells me. "I've known him my entire life. When we was kids, he was just a regular guy. Then he got a little wild. Now that his wife has passed, he's gotten a little—well, I'll just say—he ain't doin' so good."

"King of the Road" singer Roger Miller grew up in Erick. Roger Miller is gone, but another musician still lives here. That's Harley Russell, who isn't famous, though he is well featured in Route 66 guide books, which is where I found out about him and why we've made it a point to visit Erick.

WHEN THE PANCAKES AND EGGS ARE GONE and our plates are toast-mopped clean, Quincy and I wheel our bikes across the street and onto the porch of the Sand Hills Curiosity Shop. I'm not sure if it's a grocery store or an antique store or maybe even a museum. I read a battered sign: "We open when we wake up and close when we pass out!" The old door squeaks as we walk inside. It takes a few moments to drink it all in. There's antique furniture, guitars, books, photographs of some of the thousands of roadies who've stopped in over the years, and random road signs. The room is bursting, almost spilling out onto the front porch.

Also filling the room is the sound of guitar music. Harley is standing tall and strummin' loud. Grizzly looking with long gray hair and a shaggy beard, he's shirtless, sporting red and white striped overalls. A few of his teeth are missing. Right now, he's surrounded by a circle of black leather motorcycle bikers from Sweden, who sit spellbound on folding chairs, foreigners in a suddenly even more foreign land.

"I want to welcome you here to Erick, Oklahoma," Harley intones, "the redneck capital of the world, where you can see rednecks work and play in their own environment. You're in the world-famous Sand Hills Curiosity Shop. My name's Harley." Then Harley pauses, widens his eyes to take us all in, and asks, "Who the hell are you?!"

HARLEY LAUNCHES INTO HIS VERSION of the song "Route 66." I watch his left hand slide over the frets, up and down the worn neck of his ancient guitar. A few of the bikers try to keep a beat with tambourines that Harley has handed out. They clap and smile, lost in Harley's world.

His next song is different and the smiles quickly fade. Harley sings a sad, slowed-down version of the Beatles song "Yesterday." It takes on deeper meaning when we find out that he's singing about his wife, Annabelle. Although no one else in the crowded room knew her, it doesn't matter, Harley's sorrow comes through with every line:

Yesterday, all my troubles seemed so far away…

Annabelle had come to town in 1987 to visit her grandparents—a slender woman with long, silky hair. She walked into Harley's shop, hoping he'd tune her guitar—and never left. Through the years she sang every song with Harley, standing right next to him, greeting every tourist who walked through the doors with a smile and a free cold drink.

Harley posted this on his Facebook page a couple of years ago:

> "Dear friends, my Precious Annabelle just passed away 1:10 p.m. this afternoon Sept. 30, 2014. Thank all of you for everything you have done."

There's sorrow woven into every word that Harley sings.

*Now it looks as though they're here to stay. /
Oh, I believe in yesterday.*

A COUPLE OF SONGS LATER, the group from Sweden is back on their motorcycles, revving up to leave. Harley rushes outside and stands in the street, waving a huge Swedish flag as if he's starting the Indy 500. The bikers wave as they roar past, heading back toward Route 66. When the last one is gone and the reverberations from their engines have faded, Harley stands alone in the middle of the hot street in this near-empty town.

He slowly walks back inside to get ready for the next group of tourists that may roll into the Sand Hills Curiosity Shop.

EASY MORNINGS

IT'S ALWAYS DIFFICULT FOR QUINCY and me to get an early start. Maybe that's because we're staying in too many motels where crisp white sheets have a really high thread count. Maybe it's because of the free breakfast, and our habit of dragging out our refueling time by stacking yet another layer of bacon onto a third waffle before drinking just one more glass of orange juice, always aware that we should have been on the road an hour ago. Maybe it's because our tired bodies still haven't fully recovered from yesterday's ride.

Every worn tread has earned its place. Every patch on our tubes is a medal of honor.

WHEN WE DO FINALLY PUSH OFF and settle into our saddles, the mornings are my favorite part of the day's ride. My energy is renewed, and I'm thrilled to be back on the bike. In the desert, in the mountains, in the farmlands of the Midwest, mornings are always magical. The day is new, the air is fresh, and we usually manage to ride on quiet roads. The occasional car or pickup almost always slows down as it approaches and then navigates a careful, wide arc around us.

The sun rises gold and warm off to the right. My chain is purring in the sprockets and our tires sing over the pavement.

Our tires are becoming smooth with wear. We don't care. We like them that way. Every nick in a tire tells a small story. Every worn tread has earned its place. Every patch on our tubes is a medal of honor.

Hours pass, and the shadows of our bikes faithfully follow

— EASY MORNINGS —

along beside us before slowly moving under our wheels. I am fully aware that someday this time with my son will be a distant memory. I often glance over at Quincy, marveling at who he's become. "I love ya, Dude."

"I love ya too, Dad."

He takes both hands off his handlebars, sits up straight, and pedals...

QUINCY MIGHT REACH DOWN TO GRAB his caged water bottle and take a swig, which reminds me to hydrate, so I place my Camelback's plastic tube into my mouth and suck. I glance into the tiny mirror that extends a few inches out from my sunglasses and notice a pickup approaching. Instinctively, I drop in line behind Quincy and follow his trusted back wheel. The pickup swings wide around us and moves on down the road.

Quincy reaches around blindly to the back of his Camelback. His hand knows right where to find the outside pocket and extract our creased map. He takes both hands off his handlebars, sits up straight, and pedals as he studies it. His bike stays on course, like a trusty steed. I watch Quincy's hand return the map back to its pocket, somehow knowing exactly where to reach. A few seconds later, Quincy is second-guessing himself. He reaches for the map again to verify our route. My stomach tells me that a meal stop can't be far away.

WHERE HOOTERS —*is a*— FAMILY RESTAURANT

— THE ROAD BETWEEN US —

WHEN WE CROSS THE BORDER into Texas, it feels as though we have pedaled into another country. Many folks here don't think of themselves as Americans. They think of themselves as Texans.

Texans are some of the friendliest people I've ever met. Right after the state line, a huge blue sign greets us with what could be the state mantra: "Drive Friendly—The Texan Way." Almost every passing pickup driver waves and nods "howdy." Given half a chance, most will gladly lend a helping hand.

We're hot and hungry, and I've got a flat tire. We find some shade and banter while we work on it. In a short time, the patched tire is back on the bike. Now, smeared with grease and grit, we're starving. There's a restaurant close by.

IT'S A HOOTERS. Seriously? I'm a little out of my comfort zone going into Hooters, especially with my son. But there's little energy left to look for another place to eat, and after all, we're in Texas, which has it own rules about what is normal.

Neither of us has been in a Hooters before. (At least, that's what Quincy tells me and what I tell him.) We swing open the door, expecting to be greeted by a Penthouse model with pole dancers in the background. Instead, it looks like just another Denny's. Families fill the place. Young children color their placemats. Yes, the waitresses are wearing the standard-issue orange short shorts with suspenders and white T-shirts. Yes, it says "Hooters" right there on their chests. But these are not the girls you might expect. And that's enough detail for this book, except to say that our waitress greeted us with a smile as big as her Texas-sized belly and as bright as her red TRUMP hat.

— WHERE HOOTERS IS A FAMILY RESTAURANT —

OUR NEXT ROADSIDE ATTRACTION IS the Cadillac Ranch, which locals call one of the Seven Wonders of Texas. In 1976, a wealthy Texas rancher named Stanley Marsh commissioned a few Bay Area artists to bury several Cadillacs nose first in one of his fields. Every day, dozens of tourists make the pilgrimage to take photos of this rusting line of "art." Many bring along a can of spray paint to add their autograph on top of those of a thousand earlier visitors.

> *"We don't call 911. Why call? Just aim!"*

Down the road is the Cadillac Ranch RV Park, with its own row of Cadillacs, though these are still shiny and parked. Towering high is a giant statue of a cowboy wearing a bright yellow shirt with "2nd Amendment Cowboy" inscribed on the front. It's neither paranoid nor unrealistic to assume that pretty much everyone here is packing heat.

Some folks in Texas name their kids Nugget or Rifle. A few miles back we passed a home flying the rebel flag. At the entrance of another gravel driveway we spotted a big welcome sign displaying a rifle and these words: "We don't call 911. Why call? Just aim!"

Outside Amarillo is another must-see destination: a restaurant–more like a feedlot–called The (World Famous) Big Texan Steak Ranch, where they offer patrons a free 72-ounce steak dinner

— WHERE HOOTERS IS A FAMILY RESTAURANT —

— THE ROAD BETWEEN US —

if they can eat the entire meal in less than an hour. A local told me that he and his family once watched a patron get "this close!" before barfing all over the table.

Restaurant Rule #7:
"Should you become sick, the contest is over. YOU LOSE!
(Please use the container provided as necessary.)"

We pedal our way across the vast expanse that is Texas, constantly surprised by what lies around each corner.

MISSOURI:
WHERE EVERY CHICKEN IS NAMED BOB

— THE ROAD BETWEEN US —

RIDING INTO PARTS OF OUR COUNTRY that till now Quincy and I have only read about expands our understanding of who we are as Americans. In Missouri, we discover a culture molded by explorers and by the early settlers who plowed the rich soil and struggled to make the wilderness their new home. Think Lewis and Clark. Mark Twain. Harry Truman. And the Wehde family.

— MISSOURI: WHERE EVERY CHICKEN IS NAMED BOB —

Yesterday we were pedaling through soaking rain and didn't know a single person in the entire state. Tonight we're the honored guests of the Wehdes. Their warmth and kindness makes us feel like we'd be welcome to move in for a month.

We sit with the family around an outdoor dinner table. The kids listen intently to our bicycle stories as we enjoy a dinner of the best ribs I've ever tasted. Tom's wife, Sarah, touches my shoulder, "Can I get you some more?"

"If I could order up the rain, I'd ask for an inch every Sunday."

THIS FEELS LIKE HOME. The stories go on and I feel myself relaxing in the glow of their hospitality, realizing that I've been lonely for home. An orange sun rakes over endless fields of green corn, then slowly sinks. Fireflies begin to twinkle over a perfect lawn. A neighbor turns off his riding lawn mower and walks over for a beer. Grandpa tells stories of playing baseball in the 1950s. "Pitching back then was simple. All my catcher had to do was point his one finger down the middle."

The dinner conversation bounces from the need for more rain to the price of various crops to hunting and fishing. "If I could order up the rain, I'd ask for an inch every Sunday. Then I

— MISSOURI: WHERE EVERY CHICKEN IS NAMED BOB —

wouldn't have to work the fields Monday," Tom jokes. "I farm because I love it. When the planting season starts, I can do it all day long. But when hunting season starts, I'll hunt every day."

Neighbor Jesse sips on his beer and shares his thoughts about farming. "My father taught me how to plant when I was 14. He came to check my progress after a couple of hours and pointed out that my rows were crooked. He was real proud of his straight rows. But instead of getting mad, he just told me to make every row in the field straighter than the one before. I didn't know it at the time, but that's been a life lesson I've always tried to live by. I try to make every day better than the day before; I try to keep my rows straight."

OUR CONVERSATION SOMETIMES CIRCLED BACK to great-great grandpa, Captain Wehde, who sailed from Germany and came up the Mississippi in 1840. This family has been farming here ever since. Grandma is famous for her cherry pie and proud of her 30 grandkids and 30 great-grandkids. Her Christmas dinners often bring 100 family members to her table. A lot of the extended family live close by. Some live right next door.

The dad pulls out his cell phone and shows us photos of a huge catfish he hooked. The living room walls display mounted trophies of ducks, turkeys, and deer. Family photos and paintings chronicle generations of family.

— MISSOURI: WHERE EVERY CHICKEN IS NAMED BOB —

I ASK ABOUT GUNS, wanting to understand why there are so many gun clubs, gun shops, and shooting ranges. Fourteen-year-old Charlie says, "When you talk about guns in Missouri, people's first reaction is 'hunting.'" It's a skill that's been handed down over the generations. Charlie's younger sisters learned to hunt and shoot by the time they turned eight.

The girls are members of the local 4-H club. Every year they raise chickens—each of which they name Bob—and hogs to sell at auction. $1,500 is a good price for a hog. The profit goes straight into their college fund. They are also skilled s'mores chefs. Natalie, a fourth grader, stokes the small bonfire. The orange sparks, like tiny fish, swim up to the sky. She turns to me and says, "Golden brown, golden brown, that's how I like my marshmallows. Can I get you another one?"

THE ROAD BETWEEN US

CAFÉ CULTURE

JUST ABOUT EVERY TIME WE GO into a coffee shop, we discover a small group of old guys (as in, my age) sitting around a table for their morning chitchat. Back in La Jolla, California, where I live part-time, I heard them talking about their financial investments. In Ashland, Oregon, they discuss

— CAFÉ CULTURE —

who they were in past lives. In New Mexico, I listened to a long conversation about the price of dirt. In Oklahoma, it was the weather and the price of cattle.

> *All four of them have lived in this small town for nearly 70 years.*

THIS MORNING, IN A COFFEE SHOP in Bourbon, Missouri, a group of four friends are talking about their buddy Daryl, whose claim to fame is that he drove his lawn mower four hours to a neighboring town 29 miles away and back. All four of them have lived in this small town for nearly 70 years. One worked in a lead mine. Another salvaged scrap metal. Fred grew up in Leesburg. He describes one of his friends, Raymond, as "a grade A mechanic, and a great person." Raymond's brother, Dale, is also a mechanic. He has lived here all his life. Ray assures me that his friends are all "pretty good boys."

You can't deny the friendship. I wonder how many sophisticated folks would dismiss these guys without understanding the way they feel about each other. You get that they'd be there for each other in a pinch, no matter what. We say our good-byes. I pedal on, feeling the high of having been welcomed to their clan as a respected visitor.

on
OUR
WAY
— *to* —
NOWHERE

— THE ROAD BETWEEN US —

ON THIS TRIP, MY SON AND I ARE ADRIFT. We wander happily, without care or purpose. We take rest days, parking our bicycles in a motel room and taking in a movie or checking out a bike shop. Sometimes we amble through huge mall parking lots or walk aimlessly in the cooling dusk through a middle-American neighborhood alive with the scent of fresh-cut grass. We pass Craftsman-style homes where the family sits on the wraparound porch watching us. We often have no clue exactly where we are, and we don't care. There's no time clock to punch, no school bell to call us in from recess, no curfew to observe.

I tapped into this feeling back when we were crossing the Mojave, a desert so vast that I imagined I could stand on a bucket and see tomorrow; I was often tempted to lay my bike down and meander out to just sit and be.

We are not misplaced; we are not missing. This sense so permeates the trip that it sustains me the day I lose sight of Quincy. For hours.

THAT DAY, WE WERE CROSSING NEW MEXICO, where much of Route 66 has been replaced by a modern highway. I know Quincy is somewhere behind me. I keep glancing back and finally stop to wait patiently on the freeway shoulder, under a blowtorch of heat that drives me into the meager shade of a speed limit sign with a big 70 on it. I lean my bicycle against the sign, which vibrates in the traffic's wind. Minutes pass, heavy like the semitrucks that thunder the blacktop with their burdensome loads. I wait.

I try to reach Quincy on my phone. No answer. I squint down the

— THE ROAD BETWEEN US —

— ON OUR WAY TO NOWHERE —

— ON OUR WAY TO NOWHERE —

interstate, searching for movement in the distance. My parental worry activates, filling my head with gory "what-ifs." I speed-dial him again. And again. I consider hopping on my bike and backtracking against the traffic. Instead, I make myself relax and sit down on the side of the hard road, my back to the traffic a few yards away. I feel the anxiety drain from my body as trust replaces it. An hour later, my phone blinks to life with a welcoming text: "Dad, there's something wrong with my axle. I think I got it fixed. On my way."

"Sorry, Dad. I was in a cell hole."

A train moves across the horizon and lets out a trumpet of honks. Nearby, prairie dogs bark and eyeball me while nervously darting in and out of their holes in the red-brown dirt. The day melts into late afternoon. I squint again up the long interstate and finally see the familiar outline of my son on his bike. A trucker whizzes past, and I tilt my head skyward, silently mouthing, "Thank you, God."

QUINCY HAS A STREAK OF BLACK grease smeared across his forehead. He rolls up, apologizing. "Sorry, Dad. I was in a cell hole. My axle, actually my wheel skewer, is busted." He shows me how he repaired it with a short length of plastic zip tie.

— ON OUR WAY TO NOWHERE —

— ON OUR WAY TO NOWHERE —

He sits down next to me on the warm black asphalt, taking swigs from his plastic water bottle. We're both tired but happy to be reunited. I turn to him and smile. "You know, Quincy, there's something nice about just sitting on the side of an interstate in the middle of nowhere. It's a different kind of fun."

A NOTHER PRAIRIE DOG POPS ITS HEAD out of a hole in the dirt to check out this new stranger. Quincy takes another swing and surveys the scene. "It sure is, Dad."

The moment freezes like the snap of a photo. It's perfect. Why? We're present. We're just here in the middle of nowhere, which, as I suddenly remember, can also be spelled "now here."

when the
JOURNEY
is more
IMPORTANT
than the
DESTINATION

— THE ROAD BETWEEN US —

I**T'S ANOTHER BLISTERING HOT DAY ON ROUTE** 66. Quincy and I have pedaled over 70 miles and are nearing Tucumcari, New Mexico, most of it on frontage roads paralleling I-40. The interstate sits high here, elevated on a broad dirt berm.

We've been noticing frequent single-lane cement tunnels positioned below the interstate to allow small cars and farm tractors to get to the other side without obstructing highway traffic. By the look of the brown mud stains high up on the tunnel walls, they also serve as escape routes for flash floods.

> *The birds dart in and out of the tunnel in a nervous panic…*

We ride our loaded bikes into one of these tunnels, down a narrow drive and deep under the freeway. Our wheels splash through a long puddle at the tunnel entrance, and a thin stream of red mud immediately coats our tires. The tunnel shudders as semitrucks roar overhead.

FINDING A DRY PATCH OF GROUND, we lean our bikes against the concrete wall. I wonder how many gully-washers have purged through here, blowing out the other end as if from a gigantic firehose. We notice several swallow nests in a long row, like tiny mud apartments, running along the crease where the high wall meets the ceiling. The birds dart in and out of the tunnel in a nervous panic, wondering if these human intruders might be a serious threat.

This place provides sanctuary from a day of extreme heat; a

cooling breeze moving through the tunnel gently sweeps over us, and we pace back and forth to stretch our sore muscles. I turn, lean my back against the cool concrete, and slowly slide down to a squat. My chapped lips sip on a plastic water bottle, my dehydrated cells anxious for the life-giving liquid. The wall vibrates against my back from the traffic overhead. Moments pass, and the quart of water and the snack begin to work their magic. I've interrupted the dehydration cycle.

WE BANTER NOW, NOT LIKE A FATHER AND SON but like two crusty farmhands with Okie accents, characters in *The Grapes of Wrath*. Before long, we erupt in laughter, which bounces around the cement walls and out the tunnel with the scurrying birds.

The swallows soon return, calm now, and peek down at us from their mud homes. I wonder if they'd agree with my sudden insight: when the journey is better than the destination, you know you're in good company.

A
NEW
WORLD
CHAMPION

QUINCY DESCRIBES IT LIKE THIS: "It's a look of the eye—and the race is on!"

There's often a natural competitiveness between fathers and sons. Often, even near the end of a long day, Quincy and I race each other up the last few hills. While my e-bike gives me a slight head start, as my speed nears the 20-mph mark, whatever assistance my bike is giving me is programmed to shut off. Now I'm on my own, and it's a struggle to maintain the lead. As my heart and lungs are about to explode and my tongue is dragging in my spokes, Quincy eases ahead. He raises his arms in triumph, and I smile inside as I see this mirror image of myself at age 23 whizz by, celebrating.

As a young boy, Quincy balked at wearing a seatbelt so I made a contest out of it. Whoever got in car and fastened his seat belt first had to be called champ for the rest of the day. Of course, whenever I won he called me chimp! More than a few times, he would excuse himself from a restaurant table and sneak off to the car, piling his books and backpack on my seat to slow me down. That contest went on for years until one day when I dashed off the front porch of our local coffee shop to get to my seat first, snapped my calf muscle, and ended up in the ER.

We also used to wrestle. Once, when Quincy was about eight, he jumped up in the air to perform his Hulk Hogan body slam on me and came down so hard that the bed broke, splintering into pieces on the floor.

DURING MY FIRST BIKE TRIP ACROSS America in 1976, a friend and I had so many flats that we held timed contests to see who could take off a tire, find the leak, patch the tube,

— A NEW WORLD CHAMPION —

and reinflate the tire to 80 psi in record time. (It's funny how a bicycle can provide exercise even when you're off it.) On this trip, Quincy remembered how I used to brag about the record I held for many years: 10 minutes, 32 seconds. So when he got a flat, he insisted that I get out the timer. I have rarely seen him so focused and determined.

BY THE TIME I HAVE THE TIMER IN HAND and say "go," he has his tools methodically laid out on the blacktop. He's got the rear wheel off his bike and has pulled out the tube with one yank. Remarkably, he finds the puncture immediately and applies glue to the trouble spot. I do my best, unsuccessfully, to distract him.

"Got enough glue on that tube? Are you sure there aren't more holes?"

The seconds tick. In spite of the 100-degree heat and intense humidity, he works with the efficiency of a skilled surgeon. As he inflates the tire his right hand is like a jackhammer on the pump. He quickly snaps his tire gauge onto the valve and proclaims, "Yes! 80 psi exactly!" The clock nears the 10-minute mark, but he already has the wheel back on. At exactly 10 minutes, 10 seconds, his bike is standing upright. Quincy's arms shoot up into the air, and the new champion lets the world know it: *"I am the greatest!"*

A passing semitruck blasts its horn. The torch has been passed.

THIRST

— THE ROAD BETWEEN US —

I**T'S JULY BY THE TIME WE REACH OKLAHOMA,** and getting an early start is more important than ever. Getting on our bikes just after sunrise means we get to ride for a while in the cooler morning air. Sometimes I bring out my iPhone and play music, often without using my earbuds. The music is never very loud, and the country roads are empty and quiet anyway. Willy Nelson's voice drifts along with us as we roll past country farms. Bright green stalks of corn stand contrasted against old, weathered barns. A rusty windmill squeaks as it tries to turn in a failing breeze.

Willy strums "On the Road Again." "*Like a band of gypsies, we go down the highway. We're the best of friends, insisting that the world turns our way.*" Right when he sings, "We're the best of friends," my son pedals his bike in close and puts his hand on my shoulder.

ONCE THE SUN STARTS TO CLIMB, the air becomes dry and still. We push through it. I usually hate headwinds, but on these mornings I wish we had one—anything to brush some of the heat off our bodies. I remind myself to take sips from the tiny hose that leads to my Camelback. Most nights, I empty a couple of packets of Emergen-C into the water bladder, then cram the Camelback into the motel room's small refrigerator. The following morning, the water stays cool until about 10 a.m. I rarely drink enough of it.

As I bicycle through the heat one morning, the sun slow-cooks me like a Sunday roast. During the first few hours my body's cooling system is efficient, keeping me at an even temperature. But eventually the sweat begins at my forehead, small drops at first, soon becoming a steady stream down my reddened face.

— THIRST —

The air moves over my skin and lifts moisture out of my pores. Every breath expels additional moisture. I take a sip from the Camelback hose. The water's no longer cool, but at least it's wet. I think I'm replacing the water that is being sucked out of my body. It is never enough.

Some 50 to 75 percent of the human body is water. It's the one thing no plant or animal can survive without. Life empties out when the water is gone.

BEFORE I LEFT ON THIS TRIP, I discussed hydration with two physician friends. Both talked at length about the cellular wall, a semipermeable membrane something like a soft contact lens, dependent on liquid. When the membrane becomes water starved, it hardens. Nutrients no longer pass through it with ease. Cellular functions are compromised. Organ functions slow. Joints lack lubrication. Muscles tighten. Blood volume falls. Blood pressure increases. The brain, made up of 85 percent water and sensitive to even small changes in levels of ions like sodium and potassium, begins to shrink. Oxygen has a difficult time reaching the brain. Neurotransmitters, which carry the messages from one neuron to another, become depleted. Cognitive skills slow. Confusion takes hold. Brain fog drifts in, often followed by depression. The body's normally efficient thermostat begins to fail. Organs start shutting down to conserve energy for survival. The body slowly enters a state of crisis.

The heat that morning seems to come from inside the earth. Here and there we see steam oozing out of the dirt and creating a wispy layer of fog. Around 11:00 a.m., I feel sluggish. "Quincy," I say, "I don't know what's wrong with me. I just can't seem to get moving. I feel like I'm out of gas."

The sadness tightens its grip, relentless…

BY 11:30 A.M., OUR USUAL PATTERN OF RIDING together changes. Soon Quincy is far ahead. My wheels slow. A sadness sweeps in and folds over me. My wheels barely turn, then slow to a crawl. Quincy's tail light is now a tiny red dot ahead. My bike stops. My feet plant themselves on the hot blacktop as I straddle the bike. Quincy's blinking light, like a red heartbeat, beckons, encouraging me to keep going. I take a deep breath, put my right foot on the pedal, and push forward.

With Quincy still far ahead, we pass through another no-name town. I beg the gods to find a café where we can take refuge. Traffic creeps past, slowing as it moves through town, pinning me closer to the curb. My brain barely notices the loud trucks spewing black smoke, their multi-sets of trailer wheels rolling just inches away.

My bike takes me to a patch of dirt on the side of the road. Once again, my wheels roll to a stop, this time refusing to go farther.

My shoes touch down. My arms lean forward onto the handlebars. The sadness tightens its grip, relentless as the midday heat. My eyes lose sight of Quincy's blinking light and look down at the top of my front tire, worn smooth from so many miles. My head lowers and rests on my arms. Tears fill my eyes, brimming, finally breaking the levee of my lids to stream down my face. My stomach tightens. The wailing creeps up from deep within. Slow at first, it soon becomes a steady gush of uncontrollable surrender.

CARS SLOW. I TURN MY HEAD and see drivers lean over their steering wheels to have a look. Unable to take it all in, they roll past.

Tears flow. Snot empties from my nose.

Then I feel arms around my shoulders, gentle and reassuring, like the wings of an angel.

My son. My son. My son.

Quincy leads me to a nearby picnic table under some trees. I crawl on top and curl up on it like a piece of Carolina shrimp. He dashes off to find a bottle of green Gatorade. The wooden tabletop, which should feel rock hard, has the softness of a Ritz-Carlton mattress. I sink into it. My heart slows. A soothing breeze blows through the trees. My eyes close. My tears dry, leaving tiny rivulets of salt. I think I'm going to be okay.

CROSSING
—*the*—
BIG
MUDDY

— THE ROAD BETWEEN US —

MISTY FOG CIRCLES US AS WE CROSS the Mississippi over the Chain of Rocks Bridge. Spanning the river at the north end of St. Louis, Chain of Rocks gets its name from the river's rocky shoal south of the bridge. Nearby, water intake towers stand in the river like half-submerged castle turrets.

The bridge, built in 1929, is just over a mile in length, one of the longest continuous steel truss bridges in America. As we pedal across, I wonder about the first planning meetings way back then, envisioning a bridge that could span the broad Mississippi River, hold up to heavy traffic, resist spring flooding, and still allow ships to pass under it. What an engineering feat! It carried motor traffic across the river for four decades, then was superceded by pair of larger, wider bridges constructed just to the north. Now Chain of Rocks carries only pedestrians and bicyclists.

QUINCY AND I TAKE OUR TIME ON THAT BRIDGE, stopping often to lean over the side and watch the mass of brown water passing underneath, flowing with a slow yet powerful determination—winding, bending, surging toward the Gulf of Mexico. We knew that traversing the Mississippi would be a benchmark for us, a moment we'd be proud of, yet now we hesitate to celebrate. It's a trophy all right; we've bicycled over 2,500 miles together, but it's also a reminder. We sense what we don't speak—that we're getting closer to the end of our trip.

Rain comes as we coast down the bridge's slope onto the shores of Illinois. Our foul weather gear keeps us dry but traps a dank humidity that keeps our clothes moist. We need to find refuge.

Even though we haven't pedaled many miles today, we need a break. The pile of carbs we ate at sunrise is long gone. Many transcontinental bikers will tell you that one of their favorite

times of the day is second breakfast. We spot the bright yellow and black sign: Waffle House.

Quincy and I park our bicycles under the restaurant's overhang, against the large glass windows. Inside, we slide into a booth from where we can keep an eye on our bikes, which wait for us like faithful horses.

The place is nearly empty. We glance around for a wall plug and can't find one. Quincy checks his phone (probably for texts from girlfriends). An African American man stands at the register with a big smile, exuding the confident body language of a manager. The man at the grill wears a grease-stained apron harnessing his broad belly. Quincy and I ask for our usual—a stack of pancakes with a side of bacon and fried eggs.

Quincy smooths out the Adventure Cycling map on the table to check our progress and plot the course for the rest of the day. Our redheaded waitress pours hot coffee. We dump in the cream and stir it slowly—round and round—in the same rhythm as our bicycle pedals. Quincy continues his texting ritual as I pretend not to watch the Waffle House crew interact.

They banter back and forth, joking and laughing. The large guy at the grill has a sense of humor that flows so smoothly he could make reciting the Declaration of Independence sound funny. He goes into a monologue about the pros and cons of dating white women versus black women. And that's enough detail on that for this book.

These guys are tight with each other. I notice the manager, the boss, keeping a wary eye out for what's appropriate, conscious of the customers, like the guy sitting at the counter, pretending to read the newspaper and trying to constrain his belly from jiggling with laughter. But the boss relaxes, enjoying the banter, and all of us are chuckling. We've been welcomed into their circle, out here somewhere in Middle America.

"Please, dude, give it a break."

I GET A FAMILIAR FEELING IN MY GUT: I must take their portrait. Quincy senses that familiar energy and glances up from his iPhone. He rolls his eyes. "Dad…" is all he has to say. My memory fills in the rest: "Not now, not here. Please, dude, give it a break." Of course, there's a layer of subtext: "Please don't embarrass me."

It takes only a few minutes to organize the trio on the other side of the counter. I'm on a stool, camera in hand, directing them into various poses, treating them like fashion models. At first, they are clearly bewildered. Then they crack up. That's when I snap the shutter.

Quincy smiles, shakes his head, and goes back to texting, probably thinking of the time a newlywed couple on a California beach made the mistake of asking me to snap just one photo of them on their phone. A few minutes later, they found themselves in the middle of a photo shoot. Quincy still talks about that.

Sorry, son. I just can't help it.

I FINISH THE SHOOT AND WE ORDER DESSERT, lingering with our new friends and watching out the window as dark clouds empty their buckets of rain. By the time we've had another cup of coffee and the pancake syrup is mopped dry, the rain eases. Reluctantly, we say good-bye. Their laughter follows us out the door.

We ride our loaded bicycles like kids through every brown puddle in the gravel parking lot toward the bike trail, and within minutes we are pedaling along a bike path that tunnels through the forest and takes us over small, planked bridges. We turn onto an old road and glide past wet farms with their fields of tall green corn. Rabbits pivot their heads to watch us, briefly dart alongside, then scamper to hide deep in the damp shadows of the stalks.

Something has changed, and we both feel it. We're closing in on the end of our adventure together.

the
END
—*of so*—
MANY
THINGS

— THE ROAD BETWEEN US —

DURING THE PAST FEW DAYS, Quincy and I have stalled, delayed, postponed the inevitable end of our trip. Normally, anything under 50 miles of daily progress leaves us feeling guilty. Now, 25 miles or less is just fine.

Our only sense of urgency is to ask time to crawl—as if begging the ticking hand of the stopwatch on *60 Minutes* to hesitate before leaping the gap to the next second. But that's like asking for the tick without the tock. The finish line inches closer. We linger at meal stops, take longer to pack our bikes. We stay up late and wake up late. We can't freeze time, but maybe we can slow it down.

The road takes us through the South Side of Chicago, its streets littered with broken glass, houses falling apart. We know about the violence here but avoid the 24-hour news cycle and reports of daily shootings on these very corners. We treat it like any part of any other town we have traveled through.

I SPOT AN ELDERLY MAN SITTING on the crumbling cement curb and roll up to him. Asking for directions usually starts a conversation. He looks us over, as if we were from another country or maybe another planet. "What are you guys doin' here?"

When I tell him we're on our last day of a bicycle trip from LA, he just tilts his head back and stares, struggling to make sense of this. When I ask directions, he smiles and waves his hand in the general direction of the Windy City.

As we get closer to the end of the trail, Quincy takes a right off the main road, yelling, "Shortcut!" I think: here we go, on our way to getting lost again. It wouldn't be the first time. But now I don't care if we end up back in Kansas.

*We can't find a passage around the
fence and it's too tall to get over.*

We're supposed to be near the Great Lakes waterfront, but instead we're on a narrow, muddy path meandering around a small lake that soon looks more like a swamp or at least a wetland. We are indeed lost.

We are stopped by a tall cyclone fence with a two-lane road on the other side, crowded with traffic. We can't find a passage around the fence and it's too tall to get over. We can't even find a hole to squeeze our bikes through. We seem trapped.

Or are we? I straddle my bike, actually pretty happy to be exactly here by this swamp. I'm not trapped. I'm right here, right now, with my son. In that moment of appreciation, my brain activates.

"Quincy! Google Earth!" Click, click, click on my iPhone. Suddenly we can see where we are and how to find our way back to Route 66.

A MUDDY TRAIL TAKES US BACK TO THE ROAD. Now Quincy takes his map out and guides us toward the Chicago Lakefront Trail, which borders Lake Michigan—the end point of our journey up Route 66. A few blocks later, a Lycra elitist, dressed like an alien from Planet Neon, speeds by on his new titanium widget. He looks as if he's competing in the Tour de France on his lunch hour. He notices Quincy, shirtless, and yells, "Get your shirt on!"

And now, after 2,700 miles, this guy, another bicyclist, delivers the first bit of road rage.

What? I'm immediately pissed off. During the entire trip, only about five or six cars have honked at us in frustration, usually trying to pass on narrow roads. And now, after 2,700 miles, this guy, another bicyclist, delivers the first bit of road rage.

I'm ready to tear after him. But what would I do if I caught this guy? Yell back at him? Tell him he's an asphalt idiot?

I rehearse every insult I can think of but keep pedaling forward.

I'm digging, burrowing inside my anger. A mile or so later, I get it. I'm not angry about him at all. He just triggered a realization that the buzzer is actually going to sound today, signaling the end of this epic journey with my son and the end of an era for me: this will be my last cycling adventure across America.

QUINCY IS OBLIVIOUS TO ALL THIS. He rides far ahead of me, as he often does, and I'm sure he's long forgotten all about the shouting cyclist. Quincy doesn't have a short fuse like I do. He's got his focus on the next prize.

As the lake comes into view, I relax and close my eyes for just a moment. A warm summer breeze touches my face as it blows over this vast body of water. Wind rakes its surface, fashioning tiny waves that merge with other waves and ripple together toward shore. Sailboats sail. Swimmers swim. And a proud dad slows his bike. I'm not tired. I'm not dehydrated or even hungry. I'm just crying.

the WIND *in our* SAILS

A FEW DAYS BEFORE WE ROLLED INTO Chicago, Quincy and I were talking about where we might stay on our final night of the trip. He suggested looking online to see what Airbnb had to offer. To our surprise, we found a guy who rented out his trimaran sailboat anchored in middle of the harbor.

It seemed like the perfect place to spend our last night, on the water under the lights of the city skyscrapers.

The owner, a young architect named Jeff, met us at the harbor and helped us load our bikes onto a tender that motored us past innumerable yachts, until we found his 27-foot refurbished sailboat. We told Jeff about some of our sailing adventures and how Quincy is now a professional yacht captain. Jeff himself had limited experience sailing in open water and welcomed the sudden opportunity to take his boat out with two experienced sailors on board.

The wind was blowing strong that day. By the time we cleared the breakwater, whitecaps dotted Lake Michigan. Quincy and I have both done a lot of ocean sailing. This lake seemed like an ocean, with miles of open water ahead of us.

QUINCY WAS JUST FIVE YEARS OLD the first time I took him out sailing on my 16-foot Hobie Cat on an Oregon mountain lake. He sat on my lap wearing an orange life jacket so big that it came up over his ears. A few yards from shore, a gust hit us hard and filled the mainsail, then spanked the jib. The boom swung to a stop, and the mast leaned over as the rigging tightened. The Hobie Cat paused, shuddered, then quickly moved over the water. I gripped the sheet lead with one hand and kept the other on the tiller, while Quincy held onto my thighs, clamped between my knees. I eased out the main,

Quincy learned how to sail on our Hobie Cat as a young boy.

cautiously spilling some wind to slow us down. I didn't want my son's first voyage to be scary.

The sailboat carried us over the water, and my little boy grinned. He looked up at me with a bright smile on his face and said the most important words any dad could ever hope to hear, "This sure is fun, Dad. I sure love you."

Quincy senses a shift in the wind. One hand automatically tugs in the mainsheet…

NOW, NINETEEN YEARS LATER, on the final day of our bike trip, we're sailing again. Only this time Quincy is captaining the boat. The Hobie Cat wasn't nearly the size of this trimaran. The sails are worn thin with age, and the deck varnish is flaking from long days in the sun. The sails are full and the rigging is tight.

My son handles the tiller with the confidence of a captain twice his age. His eyes narrow as he scans the surface of the water ahead, searching for signs of threatening gusts. He's reading tea leaves from the future, charting our course into the unknown. Off to our starboard side, a large patch of water darkens as small waves swell and surge together, moving like a pack of beasts hunting.

Quincy senses a shift in the wind. One hand automatically tugs in the mainsheet, moving the line that zigzags its way through the block. Needing more line, he holds the slack between his teeth for a brief moment, then grabs more line to pull in. I smile. He's perfectly mimicking my move from all those years ago. Suddenly, with a firm snap of his wrist, he locks line into cleat with a grace that exceeds anything I ever taught him. He reaches over to pull in the jib. His other hand brings the tiller in toward his body with the easy grace of a Zen master.

BY NOW, THE SAILBOAT IS MOVING RAPIDLY, charging through whitecaps with a force strong enough to dig the leeward hull deep into the water while the windward hull begins to slowly lift out of the lake. I'm not alarmed or even concerned. I trust my son, and I love the familiar excitement, moving deep in my belly, of being in a boat under full sail. I watch Quincy safely pilot this two-ton sailboat by harnessing 20 knots of wind blowing into about 500 square feet of weathered sail. Our boat moves at a perfect angle, flying across the water. Jeff is impressed.

Clouds part to reveal the sun at its zenith in the blue sky. A shaft of golden light suddenly warms us. The hardened muscles that shape Quincy's tanned shoulders relax. He eases his grip on the line and looks over at me, smiling, knowing exactly what his dad is about to say.

"This sure is fun, Quincy. I sure love you."

— THE ROAD BETWEEN US —

POSTSCRIPT

Quincy and I are back home, sitting in my favorite coffee shop. Although my tan is fading, I haven't regained a single pound of the 12 that I shed on the trip. I fight the urge to get a toasted bagel with my cup of coffee and change that. My son has those damned white earbuds jammed into the sides of his head again and is gazing out the window, perhaps

dreaming about his next adventure, probably on a sailboat in exotic waters halfway across the world.

We spent two months together out there on Route 66. We experienced what I can only describe as complete freedom. That has now changed. Mick Dolan, a bicyclist we met from the UK, said, "Coming back is like being a piece of a jigsaw puzzle left out in the rain—it's hard to fit in." He's right. It's all too easy for one day to once again seep into the next. I'm okay with that. For a while. Maybe there will be another adventure, like wandering through India.

I'M PRETENDING TO READ THE *NEW YORK TIMES*. I hold the paper high to cover most of my face as I covertly study the window light reflecting off Quincy's face. A river of the photographs of Quincy I took through his growing-up years flows through my mind. Here's the thing: I'm still as amazed at the miracle of my son as I was 23 years ago when I gently guided him out of his mother's womb.

Quincy's head moves to the rhythm of the song that streams through the white iPhone cords. Suddenly, he yanks on the buds and they drift to his lap. He swivels to face me, tilts his head, maybe noticing the tears in my eyes, and says: "Hey, Dad, your cup is almost empty. Can I get you a refill?"

I quickly dump the paper and jump to my feet. "That's okay, dude.

— POSTSCRIPT —

I can get it myself." I stride across the floor, remembering how crossing a floor used to hurt during our biking adventure.

I FILL MY CUP AND THINK OF THE COUPLE from England who followed our blog on Facebook for the entire trip. They hold the record for the longest e-bike trip around Europe, 23,000 kilometers. They invited me to join them next year to bike around Australia. They offered to pay for everything, including a new bike.

Here's why I said no.

I know that nothing could reach the heights of my trip with Quincy. Why set myself up for a colossal disappointment?

Besides, I've learned what I needed from the road. I know now how fear can define our lives if we let it, like the fear of getting old, of disappointing your son, of failing to get up a steep hill. Fear can slam doors. We may hide inside that fear for years, never realizing that the door may indeed be closed but it's not locked. We can open that door; we can face our fear; we can say, "Hell, yes!" When we do, our lives can change.

Confronting fear is different for everyone. For you, it could mean asking the boss for a raise or speaking up about something important that everyone else is pretending isn't in the room. It might mean grabbing the microphone in front of a large crowd, clearing your throat, and risking being foolish. It could mean asking the beauty sitting two rows back to the prom, or ending a marriage that died years ago.

Courage makes us heroes. And heroes sometimes run toward the explosion instead of away from it. Remember, fear never wrote a symphony or a poem, never negotiated a peace treaty or cured a disease. Courage did that.

It takes courage to choose and define the life we want, and to make dreams happen. How do we do it? We have to risk failing. What do we stand to gain? Possibly everything.

www.ingramcontent.com/pod-product-compliance
Lightning Source LLC
Chambersburg PA
CBHW041439010526
44118CB00002B/132